SAVING THE YELLOW EYE

JOHN DARBY

CONTENTS

1. A Very Special Bird 3
2. Learning About the Yellow Eye 11
3. Counting Penguins 17
4. Helping Hands 25

A Very Special Bird

When an animal becomes extinct, the last animal of that kind dies. Sometimes people can stop this happening. But first, someone has to work out what the problem is and then solve it. The yellow-eyed penguin was in danger of dying out until people started to help.

Penguins are amazing animals. The first penguins I studied lived in the Antarctic. They were called Adelie penguins.

Later, I wanted to find out how Adelie penguins were different from penguins that lived in a warm place. So I decided to study the yellow-eyed penguin that lives in New Zealand.

The yellow eye is a very special bird. It is the rarest penguin in the world.

It used to live in big forests that grew by the sea. But these forests were cut down or burnt. The land was ploughed up to grow grass for farm animals to eat. For many years, most yellow-eyed penguins had to share their nesting areas with sheep and cows.

Penguins' nests are very hard to find. There are twenty-six nests on this beach. You have to get on your hands and knees to find most of them.

PENGUIN FACT FILE

There are 17 different kinds of penguin. They all live in the bottom half of the world – the southern hemisphere.

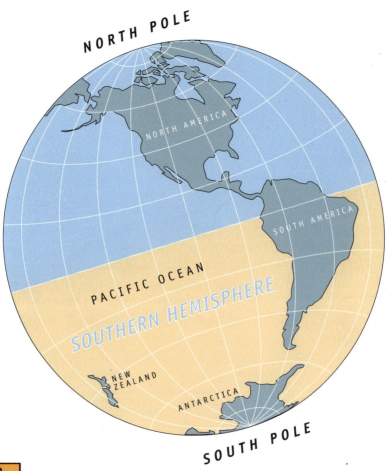

Big and Small

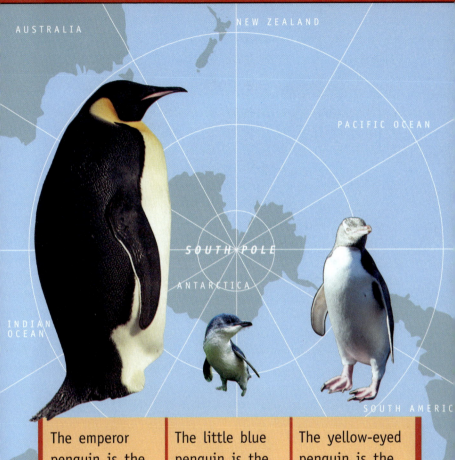

The emperor penguin is the biggest penguin in the world. It weighs about 30 kilograms.

The little blue penguin is the smallest penguin in the world. It weighs just over 1 kilogram.

The yellow-eyed penguin is the fourth largest penguin in the world. It usually weighs about 5 kilograms.

2 LEARNING ABOUT THE YELLOW EYE

Before you can help an endangered animal, you have to find out where they live and how many there are. You also study them to see how they live. When you have done that, you can work out the best way to help them.

To help scientists understand the yellow eye, we put little steel bands on the flippers of the penguin chicks. Each band has a special number on it. We put the bands on very carefully so that we don't hurt the chick. The band will usually stay there for the rest of the penguin's life.

In 1994 I made this graph about the 126 penguins I was studying. It shows the birth years of the penguins that were still alive.

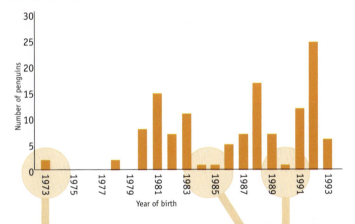

Some chicks that were banded in 1973 were still alive in 1994. This told me something important – yellow-eyed penguins can live to be over twenty years old.

But the graph also shows some problems. There was only one penguin left from 1984, one from 1985, and one from 1990.

What happened in those years?

In 1984 all the chicks in one of the nests I was studying just disappeared. The next day I went out and checked some other nests. Those chicks were gone too. I looked around and soon found a dead chick. I took it back to my laboratory to find out what had happened.

The chick had been bitten on the back of its head. The next week nearly all the chicks had been killed. A fierce little animal called a ferret was to blame.

Every year ferrets kill thousands of native birds. In 1984 and 1985 nearly all the chicks I was studying were killed before I could trap the ferrets. Very few of the penguin chicks grew up to have chicks of their own. That's what the graph shows.

In 1990 hundreds of adult penguins also died. Scientists still don't know why this happened. Without their parents, most of the chicks died too.

I was very worried about the chicks being killed and adult penguins dying. I knew that the yellow-eyed penguin could be in danger of becoming extinct.

3 COUNTING PENGUINS

For the next two years I explored many coastlines counting the penguins. I wanted to find out where *all* the yellow-eyed penguins lived and count how many there were.

I found that there were only 1200 to 1500 pairs of yellow-eyed penguins left in New Zealand and on other small islands nearby. This made the yellow eye the rarest of all the penguins in the world.

Nearly all the forests where yellow-eyed penguins had lived for millions of years had been destroyed. Everywhere I went in New Zealand, ferrets, stoats, and wild cats were killing penguin chicks.

Too many chicks were being killed. The places they lived were being destroyed. We needed to do something to stop this very special penguin becoming extinct.

To help us, we put tiny recorders on the backs of some adult penguins.

We found:
- they can dive down 120 metres to catch fish
- sometimes they do this 200 times each day
- they swim 8-10 kilometres out to deep water on most days
- sometimes they swim out over 30 kilometres!

Sometimes they have to climb steep hills and walk some distance inland to their nests.

Before people were around, the penguins didn't have to do this walking and climbing. There were cool forests right down to the sea, and the penguins could live in the shade.

23

4 HELPING HANDS

By 1987 many people were worried that the yellow eye might become extinct. They started to buy the land where the yellow eye lived.

They put up fences so that other animals couldn't get in.

They planted lots of new trees and bushes to give the penguins shelter and shade.

We set traps to catch the animals that killed penguin chicks. Students helped scientists to study the penguins. This helped us work out how we could save the yellow eye.

Now, over half the places where yellow eyes live are protected. This graph shows that the number of yellow-eyed penguins in New Zealand is growing.

This has made all the hard work worthwhile.

YELLOW-EYED PENGUIN FACT FILE

Scientific name: *Megadyptes antipodes*

Rarest penguin in the world:
1200 to 1500 pairs left
Found only in New Zealand and some small islands nearby

Habitat: Forest and shrub land

Breeding: Two eggs are laid in September or October.
Eggs hatch after 6 weeks – each chick weighs about 56 grams.
One parent guards the chick all the time until the end of December.
Chicks go to sea in February/March.
Chicks return to breed 2 to 3 years later.

Lifespan: At least 22 years